Instant PageSpeed Optimization

Optimize your website to make it faster by enhancing its speed, traffic, and bandwidth using practical and hands-on recipes

Sanjeev Jaiswal

BIRMINGHAM - MUMBAI

Instant PageSpeed Optimization

First published: September 2013

Production Reference: 1240913

Published by Packt Publishing Ltd.
Livery Place
35 Livery Street
Birmingham B3 2PB, UK.

ISBN 978-1-84969-732-3

www.packtpub.com

Credits

Author

Sanjeev Jaiswal

Reviewer

Ravindran Navaneethan

Acquisition Editor

Akram Hussain

Commissioning Editor

Neha Nagwekar

Technical Editors

Jalasha D'costa

Kapil Hemnani

Copy Editors

Mradula Hegde

Laxmi Subramanian

Project Coordinator

Amey Sawant

Proofreader

Faye Coulman

Production Coordinator

Kirtee Shingan

Cover Work

Kirtee Shingan

Cover Image

Abhinash Sahu

About the Author

Sanjeev Jaiswal is a computer graduate with four years of industrial experience and more than six years of web development experience. He extensively uses Perl and GNU/Linux for his day-to-day work and also teaches Drupal and WordPress CMS to bloggers. He has worked closely with major clients such as CSC, IBM, and Motorola mobility.

Sanjeev loves teaching technical functionalities to engineering students and IT professionals and has been teaching since 2008. He founded AlienCoders (`http://www.aliencoders.com`) based on the principle of "learning through sharing" for Computer Science students and IT professionals in 2010, which became a huge hit in India among engineering students.

He usually uploads technical videos to YouTube on his channel "AlienCoders". Sanjeev has a huge fan base on his site and on YouTube because of his simple but effective way of teaching and his philanthropic nature toward students.

I would like to thank my parents for their moral support while writing these recipes till late into the night. I would also like to express deep thanks and gratitude to my best friend Ritesh Kamal, without whose efforts this book would quite possibly not have happened.

I would also like to thank all the mentors, friends, and supporters I've had over the years, especially my mentors Senthil KS, Siva Reddy Mudiyala, Michael Mueller, Manu Zacharia, Varghees Samraj, and the entire AlienCoder's team. There is not a chance I could be writing this book today without having learned from these people. It is because of them and a few my best friends, Ranjan Pandey, Rakesh Pandey, Pradeep Pant and others, that I achieved a set of seemingly impossible goals in an incredibly short period of time.

About the Reviewer

Ravindran Navaneethan is a software engineer from Hyderabad, India. He is a B.Tech graduate from the Government College of Technology, Coimbatore. He has more than 12 years of experience in software development and currently works at United Online Software Development (India) Pvt. Ltd.

Ravindran started his career as a Windows developer and later moved on to web development. He has hands-on experience in both Windows and web development and has managed small- to mid-sized development teams. Ravindran is interested in learning new programming languages and exploring various tools and technologies.

www.PacktPub.com

Support files, eBooks, discount offers and more

You might want to visit www.PacktPub.com for support files and downloads related to your book.

Did you know that Packt offers eBook versions of every book published, with PDF and ePub files available? You can upgrade to the eBook version at www.PacktPub.com and as a print book customer, you are entitled to a discount on the eBook copy. Get in touch with us at service@packtpub.com for more details.

At www.PacktPub.com, you can also read a collection of free technical articles, sign up for a range of free newsletters and receive exclusive discounts and offers on Packt books and eBooks.

http://PacktLib.PacktPub.com

Do you need instant solutions to your IT questions? PacktLib is Packt's online digital book library. Here, you can access, read and search across Packt's entire library of books.

Why Subscribe?

- ▶ Fully searchable across every book published by Packt
- ▶ Copy and paste, print and bookmark content
- ▶ On demand and accessible via web browser

Free Access for Packt account holders

If you have an account with Packt at www.PacktPub.com, you can use this to access PacktLib today and view nine entirely free books. Simply use your login credentials for immediate access.

Table of Contents

Preface

If you are a web developer or website administrator/owner, sooner or later you will surely require the techniques to optimize your website by using various available resources, by tweaking server settings, and so on. This book will show you how to optimize the speed of your website through various common techniques.

What this book covers

Minimizing HTTP requests (Simple) shows you that lesser the number of requests, faster the website will be. This recipe will show you how to minimize such HTTP requests without hampering the website.

Adding an Expires or Cache-Control header (Simple) shows us that adding the Expires or Cache-Control header will make downloadable files cacheable and will save time in opening websites without any delay.

Following HTML standards (Simple) teaches us that by following proper HTML standards, we can reduce the number of warning and errors that browsers catch and make the website faster by using correct tags, elements, and so on.

Reducing DOM elements (Intermediate) demonstrates that the website will take less time if there are lesser DOM elements contained within it. We can reduce it significantly by removing unnecessary DOM elements through close observation.

Setting up CSS sprites (Intermediate) shows us that by using CSS codes to show images wherever required, we can save time and space. Using one large image is better than using several different images. It also shows us how to use the CSS sprites technique on it.

Enabling compression (Simple) shows us that compressing the file size over the network would reduce the time taken to send an HTTP request and get an HTTP response back.

Optimizing images (Simple) urges us to use an image format wisely. This recipe will deal with various ways to optimize an image for the site to run faster.

Minifying JavaScript and CSS files (Simple) introduces the concept of minification, which is the technique that one should use in the production of a website in order to reduce the size of the site and thus increasing its speed.

Setting up browser caching (Simple) explains that the browser cache depends more on the user than the website owner, and the Cache-Control header can be used for this purpose.

Using Apache mod_pagespeed – installing and configuring (Advanced) introduces Apache's mod_pagespeed module, which takes care of web optimization's best practices automatically after setting up and configuring properly. We will show you how to achieve it using practical examples and code.

Making favicon.ico small and cacheable (Simple) has less impact on website optimization, but it's a good habit to make favicon simple, small, and cacheable.

Avoiding redirects and Not Found errors – 301 and 404 codes (Advanced) shows that broken links, redirections, and bad requests are never good for a website's health. So, it's better that you try to minimize it.

Using the Flush Method (Intermediate) introduces flushing, which is beneficial for those websites where a lot of backend requests are sent or the frontend bears less content to display. In this recipe, we will show how to use it efficiently in your website.

Configuring ETags (Advanced) provides a mechanism to validate the specific version of a component/entity that is returned from the server side under the response header as an ETag.

Making AJAX cacheable (Intermediate) explains how we can make AJAX cacheable by adding the Expires header to the file that will be called by AJAX; for example, autoform completion.

Rules for using the CSS, JavaScript, and image files (Simple) shows the many other ways to enhance the web response, which don't fit in any of the preceding chapters appropriately.

What you need for this book

You need the following things to perform all the recipes provided in this book:

- A web browser (Firefox preferred)
- A system with minimal configuration (Windows/Linux preferred)
- Basic web development skills
- Familiarity with HTML, CSS, and TCP/IP protocols
- A text editor (Notepad++ preferred)
- Basic knowledge of networking protocols

Who this book is for

This book is for anyone who wants to know how to optimize their website to get more traffic, to reduce the size, to minimize warnings/errors, and so on. This book can prove useful to website administrators, owners, and developers who have full access to their websites to do all the listed experiments with full permission.

Conventions

In this book, you will find a number of styles of text that distinguish between different kinds of information. Here are some examples of these styles and an explanation of their meaning.

Code words in text are shown as follows: "We can do it by using `area` and `map` tags to make it work like the previous one."

A block of code is set as follows:

```php
<?php
if (substr_count($_SERVER['HTTP_ACCEPT_ENCODING'], 'gzip')

ob_start("ob_gzhandler");
  else
ob_start();
?>
```

When we wish to draw your attention to a particular part of a code block, the relevant lines or items are set in bold:

```
cache-request-directive  = "no-cache"  | "no-store"  | "max-age" "="
delta-seconds  | "max-stale" [ "=" delta-seconds  ] | "min-fresh" "="
delta-seconds  | "no-transform"  | "only-if-cached" | cache-extension
```

Any command-line input or output is written as follows:

```
alert(document.getElementsByTagName('*').length);
```

New terms and **important words** are shown in bold. Words that you see on the screen, in menus or dialog boxes for example, appear in the text like this: "Run the following command on Firebug's console under the **Script** tab on whichever website you wish to check the total number of DOM elements."

 Warnings or important notes appear in a box like this.

 Tips and tricks appear like this.

Reader feedback

Feedback from our readers is always welcome. Let us know what you think about this book—what you liked or may have disliked. Reader feedback is important for us to develop titles that you really get the most out of.

To send us general feedback, simply send an e-mail to feedback@packtpub.com, and mention the book title via the subject of your message.

If there is a topic that you have expertise in and you are interested in either writing or contributing to a book, see our author guide on www.packtpub.com/authors.

Customer support

Now that you are the proud owner of a Packt book, we have a number of things to help you to get the most from your purchase.

Downloading the example code

You can download the example code files for all Packt books you have purchased from your account at http://www.packtpub.com. If you purchased this book elsewhere, you can visit http://www.packtpub.com/support and register to have the files e-mailed directly to you.

Errata

Although we have taken every care to ensure the accuracy of our content, mistakes do happen. If you find a mistake in one of our books—maybe a mistake in the text or the code—we would be grateful if you would report this to us. By doing so, you can save other readers from frustration and help us improve subsequent versions of this book. If you find any errata, please report them by visiting http://www.packtpub.com/submit-errata, selecting your book, clicking on the **errata submission form** link, and entering the details of your errata. Once your errata are verified, your submission will be accepted and the errata will be uploaded on our website, or added to any list of existing errata, under the Errata section of that title. Any existing errata can be viewed by selecting your title from http://www.packtpub.com/support.

Piracy

Piracy of copyright material on the Internet is an ongoing problem across all media. At Packt, we take the protection of our copyright and licenses very seriously. If you come across any illegal copies of our works, in any form, on the Internet, please provide us with the location address or website name immediately so that we can pursue a remedy.

Please contact us at `copyright@packtpub.com` with a link to the suspected pirated material.

We appreciate your help in protecting our authors, and our ability to bring you valuable content.

Questions

You can contact us at `questions@packtpub.com` if you are having a problem with any aspect of the book, and we will do our best to address it.

Instant PageSpeed Optimization

Welcome to *Instant PageSpeed Optimization*. We will learn how to make our website faster by following the recipes listed in this book. We will only concentrate on those recipes that will impact the website's performance. This will include tweaking the website to perform tasks such as minimizing HTTP requests, using the CDN, following standard HTML methods, and minifying scripts and Flush methods.

Minimizing HTTP requests (Simple)

The website can be made faster in many ways, one of them being reducing requests sent to the server, which will ultimately minimize the delay. The fewer the server requests, the faster the website will be.

How to do it...

We can do it in various ways but let's concentrate on more important ones:

- **Reducing DNS lookup**: Whenever possible try to use URL directives and paths to different functionalities instead of different hostnames. For example, if a website is abc.com, instead of having a separate hostname for its forum, for example, forum.abc.com, we can have the same URL path, abc.com/forum. This will reduce one extra DNS lookup and thus minimize HTTP requests. Imagine if your website contains many such URLs, either its own subdomains or others, it would take a lot of time to parse the page, because it will send a lot of DNS queries to the server.

For example, check `www.aliencoders.com` that has several DNS lookup components that makes it a very slow website. Please check the following image for a better understanding:

> **The components are split over more than 4 domains**
>
> * aliencoders.com: 44 components, 549.2K (175.8K GZip)
> * ct1.addthis.com: 5 components, 358.8K (94.5K GZip)
> * api.iflychat.com: 8 components, 274.8K (68.7K GZip)
> * platform.twitter.com: 10 components, 489.1K (184.8K GZip)
> * apis.google.com: 4 components, 290.1K (101.8K GZip)
> * connect.facebook.net: 2 components, 358.0K (118.1K GZip)
> * www.google-analytics.com: 2 components, 37.4K (14.9K GZip)
> * s7.addthis.com: 1 component, 6.8K (2.7K GZip)
> * ajax.googleapis.com: 1 component, 78.6K (27.1K GZip)

If you really have to serve some JavaScript files at the head section, make sure that they come from the same host where you are trying to display the page, else put it at the bottom to avoid latency because almost all browsers block other downloads while rendering JavaScript files are being downloaded fully and get executed. We will discuss more of this in the *Minifying JavaScript and CSS files (Simple)* recipe. Modern browsers support DNS prefetching. If it's absolutely necessary for developers to load resources from other domains, he/she should make use of it.

The following are the URLs:

- `https://developer.mozilla.org/en/docs/Controlling_DNS_prefetching`
- `http://www.chromium.org/developers/design-documents/dns-prefetching`

- **Using combined files**: If we reduce the number of JavaScript files to be parsed and executed and if we do the same for CSS files, it will reduce HTTP requests and load the website much faster. We can do so, by combining all JavaScript files into one file and all CSS files into one CSS file. We will discuss these techniques in detail in the *Minifying JavaScript and CSS files (Simple)* recipe.

- **Setting up CSS sprites**: There are two ways to combine different images into one to reduce the number of HTTP requests. One is using the image map technique and other is using CSS sprites. What we do in a CSS sprite is that we write CSS code for the image going to be used so that while hovering, clicking, or performing any action related to that image would invoke the correct action similar to the one with having different images for different actions. It's just a game of coordinates and a little creativity with design. It will make the website at least 50 percent faster as compared to the one with a lot of images. We will discuss more on the CSS sprites concept in the *Setting up CSS sprites (Advanced)* recipe.

- **Using image maps**: Use the image map idea if you are going to have a constant layout for those images such as menu items and a navigational part. The only drawback with this technique is that it requires a lot of hard work and you should be a good HTML programmer at the least.

However, writing mapping code for a larger image with proper coordinates is not an easy task, but there are saviors out there. If you want to know the basics of the `area` and `map` tags, you can check out the *Basics on area and map tag in HTML* post I wrote at `http://www.aliencoders.com/content/basics-area-and-map-tag-html`.

You can create an image map code for your image online at `http://www.maschek.hu/imagemap/imgmap`.

If you want to make it more creative with different sets of actions and colors, try using CSS codes for image maps..

The following screenshot shows you all the options that you can play with while reducing DNS lookups:

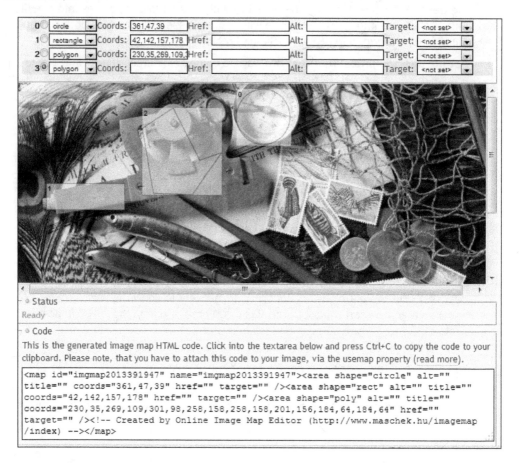

How it works...

In the case of reducing DNS lookup, when you open any web page for the first time, it performs DNS lookups through all unique hostnames that are involved with that web page. When you hit a URL in your browser, it first needs to resolve the address (DNS name) to an IP address. As we know, DNS resolutions are being cached by the browser or the operating system or both. So, if a valid record for the URL is available in the user's browser or OS cache, there is no time delay observed.

All ISPs have their own DNS servers that cache name-IP mappings from authoritative name servers and if the caching DNS server's record has already expired, it should be refreshed again. We will not go much deeper into the DNS mechanism. But it's important to reduce DNS lookups more than any other kind of requests because it will add a more prolonged latency period as any other requests do.

Similarly, in the case of using image maps, imagine you have a website where you have inserted separate images for separate tabular menus instead of just plain text to make the website catchier! For example, Home, Blogs, Forums, Contact Us, and About Us. Now whenever you load the page, it sends five requests, which will surely consume some amount of time and will make the website a bit slower too.

It will be a good idea to merge all such images into one big image and use the image map technique to reduce the number of HTTP requests for those images. We can do it by using `area` and `map` tags to make it work like the previous one. It will not only save a few KBs, but also reduce the server request from five to just one.

There's more...

If you already have `map` tags in your page and wish to edit it for proper coordinates without creating trouble for yourself, there is a Firefox add-on available called the **Image Map Editor** (`https://addons.mozilla.org/en-us/firefox/addon/ime/`).

If you want to know the IP address of your name servers, use the `$ grepnameserver / etc/resolv.conf` command in Linux and `C:/>ipconfig /all` in Windows. Even you can get the website's details from your name server, that is, `host website-name <nameserver>`. There is a Firefox add-on that will speed up DNS resolution by doing pre-DNS work and you will observe faster loading of the website. Download **Speed DNS** from `https://addons.mozilla.org/en-US/firefox/addon/speed-dns/?src=search`.

Adding an Expires or Cache-Control header (Simple)

Websites usually contain the mixture of static and dynamic elements that are being used uniformly over different pages. When a browser starts loading a web page, it usually downloads all the images, CSS files, JavaScript files, and Flash files, if any. Imagine if every time the browser had to download each and every file associated with that page, how hectic it would be for both the browser and the user, and you would have a bandwidth problem too. Gone are the days when people used few static pages with less creativity. Now, almost all websites contain a lot of JavaScript and CSS scripts; images that make the site a bit slower and heavy.

Getting ready

We can load a web page faster if we cache the images and scripts used on the website into the user's browser cache. It will only help in optimizing the website if it has been already visited and the cache is not empty, else it has no effect. The following screenshot shows which static files are required to have far future expiry dates that are cacheable:

> There are 8 static components without a far-future expiration date.
>
> - (no expires) http://platform.twitter.com/widgets.js
> - (2013/3/11) https://apis.google.com/js/plusone.js
> - (no expires) http://connect.facebook.net/en_US/all.js#xfbml=1&
> - (2013/3/12) http://www.google-analytics.com/ga.js
> - (no expires) http://s7.addthis.com/js/250/addthis_widget.js#asy
> - (no expires) http://connect.facebook.net/en_US/all.js
> - (2013/3/11) http://feeds.feedburner.com/~fc/AlienCoders?...
> - (no expires) http://www.squid-cache.org/Artwork/SN.png

How to do it...

By using the Expires headers, these components become cacheable, that is, these avoid unnecessary HTTP requests on subsequent page views. The Expires headers are most often associated with images, but they can and should be used on all page components including scripts, stylesheets, and Flash. We can do this in two ways. The first way is by using the Never Expires setting for all static components and setting the value to a far future date. If you are using a 32-bit system, better set the "expires date" till January 18, 2038, else it won't work on a 32-bit system without tweaking the code.

Add the Expires header by using the meta tag for static contents. Consider a site that requests the header with the following meta tag:

```
<META HTTP-EQUIV="Expires" CONTENT="Sat, 04 Dec 2021 21:29:02 GMT">
```

The response header would contain the Expires term like this:

```
Expires: Sat, 04 Dec 2021 21:29:02 GMT
```

Another way is by using Cache-Control metadata to assist the browser with the requests. For dynamic contents we use Cache-Control header definition like the following:

```
<META HTTP-EQUIV="CACHE-CONTROL" CONTENT="PUBLIC">
```

`Content` can be any of the four values: `public`, `private`, `no-cache`, or `no-store`. Here is some information regarding these four values:

- `public`: The content set to `public` will be cached in public-shared caches
- `private`: This content will only be cached in private cache
- `no-cache`: This content will not be cached
- `no-store`: This content will be cached but not archived

If you have Firebug enabled in your Firefox browser, you can see the `Cache-Control` header's value at the `request` and `response` header as defined in RFC 2616 (`http://www.ietf.org/rfc/rfc2616.txt`).

The following are the two cache-related header parts that you should know:

```
cache-request-directive = "no-cache"  |  "no-store"  |  "max-age" "="
delta-seconds  |  "max-stale" [ "=" delta-seconds  ]  |  "min-fresh" "="
delta-seconds   |  "no-transform"  |  "only-if-cached"  |  cache-extension
cache-response-directive ="public"  |  "private" [ "=" <"> 1#field-name
<"> ]  |  "no-cache" [ "=" <"> 1#field-name <"> ]  |  "no-store"  |  "no-
transform"  |  "must-revalidate"  |  "proxy-revalidate"  |  "max-age" "="
delta-seconds   |  "s-maxage" "=" delta-seconds
```

 For more information on the `Cache-Control` general HTML header field, please go through W3C's *Header Field Definitions* (`http://www.w3.org/Protocols/rfc2616/rfc2616-sec14.html`) under section *14.9*.

How it works...

So, when you open any website for the first time it would return status 200 and will take some time to load the page because it will download each bit of the page. It all depends on your browser settings and cookies handler options.

When you would visit the same site next time, the latency period would be much lesser and it would return the 304 status code for the scripts or files, as shown in the following screenshot:

URL	Status	Domain	Size
⊞ **GET www.aliencoders.com**	200 OK	aliencoders.com	21 KB
⊞ **POST auth**	200 OK	aliencoders.com	124 B
⊞ GET addthis_widget.js#async=1	304 Not Modified	s7.addthis.com	0 B
⊞ GET admin_menu.css?F	304 Not Modified	aliencoders.com	1.2 KB
⊞ GET css_f4bd4756dbafecd1c7671c	304 Not Modified	aliencoders.com	17.8 KB

When the status is 200, the `response` header would show how much data is downloaded for a particular request. In the following screenshot, it shows 21501 bytes under the **Content-Length** attribute:

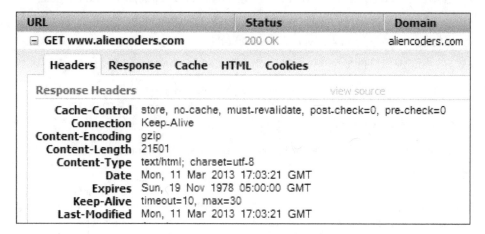

If the status code is 304, you will observe no data has been downloaded, as shown in the following screenshot:

Moreover, check the **Expires** section in the previous screenshot to get an idea of caching here.

There's more...

This `Cache-Control` header technique and the `meta` tag bearing `Expires` were introduced from HTTP/1.1 onward.

HTTP 1.1 (RFC 2068), available at `http://www.w3.org/Protocols/rfc2068/rfc2068`, specifies that all HTTP date/time stamps *must* be generated in **Greenwich Mean Time** (**GMT**) and the format should follow the rules defined in RFC 1123, that is, `weekday ","  date time "GMT"`.

- ▶ `weekday` would bear values including `Mon`, `Tue`, `Wed`, `Thu`, `Fri`, `Sat`, or `Sun`.
- ▶ `date` should be written in this format: `day`(2 digits) `month`(3 chars) `year`(4 digits). For example, 02 Jun 1982.

    The month should be represented using `Jan`, `Feb`, `Mar`, `Apr`, `May`, `Jun`, `Jul`, `Aug`, `Sep`, `Oct`, `Nov`, or `Dec`).
- ▶ `time` should be formatted as `Hour ":" Minutes":" Seconds`, which ranges from 00:00:00 to 23:59:59.

So, an example of this would be, `CONTENT="Sat, 04 Dec 2021 21:29:02 GMT"`.

Following HTML standards (Simple)

HTML is meant to display the data and you can code HTML in many ways, which will be rendered by different browsers in a different manner. So, we need some rules to be followed by all browsers to show the data uniformly. That's why we have **World Wide Consortium** (`http://www.w3.org/`) to handle this.

Getting ready

Web designers or developers should remain up-to-date with the latest technology and web standards, which include HTML5, CSS 3, JSON, and so on. Well, that doesn't mean you have to read every single specification line by line, but you will have to follow minimal web standard to achieve high percentage of uniformity of web standards over all the web browsers without losing your users.

How to do it...

If you are using HTML (not HTML5 for now), try to always write this line of code:

```
<html xmlns="http://www.w3.org/1999/xhtml" dir="ltr" lang="en-US">
```

Here, `xmlns` is the XML namespace and it should always have the value as `http://www.w3.org/1999/xhtml`. You can define in which language it should be rendered by setting the value of the `lang` attribute.

Put all the CSS files at the top under the `head` tag and try to move down all JavaScript at the bottom of the HTML code. CSS is required at the top for two reasons:

▸ To have a presentational layout as it should be

▸ So that it can be downloaded in parallel along with other HTTP requests

Use the tableless design whenever possible. The tableless forms may not make the page load faster but it will surely enhance the speed due to the following reasons:

▸ Less number of DOM elements to be parsed

▸ Layout being taken care by CSS

▸ We can use the same CSS code for more tables if present, which would save a number of lines of code and would render faster

If you are good at CSS, converting HTML table elements into a CSS layout should be a cakewalk.

Check your W3C standard validity related to HTML, CSS (mainly), and load time on a regular basis.

We shouldn't leave back any error while writing tags. It should be properly closed and you should use proper tags for the specific purpose, for example, don't use the `<b>` tag to make the string bold, rather use `<strong>`. Use proper ending methods of one-sided tags, for example, `<br />` instead of `<br>`. It would not make the site faster but will make parsing faster without any error.

We should avoid using inline JavaScript as much as possible and you should put external JavaScript files at the bottom of the HTML code. Because while downloading JavaScript files, it doesn't allow downloading anything else that will make the page load slower.

There's more...

You can follow HTML standards by analyzing errors and warnings caused by specific pages by using a Firefox add-on **HTML Validator** (`https://addons.mozilla.org/en-us/firefox/addon/html-validator/`). It has the option to check HTML and CSS validation separately online using a `w3.org` tool or by using W3C's free online validator tool (`http://validator.w3.org/`).

Results may vary from one tool to another due to analyzing error pattern difference. `<br>` may not be erroneous under HTML Tidy but it's an error under the W3C validator as it should be `<br />`.

In the following screenshot, you can see the result from HTML Validator for the URL `www.packtpub.com`:

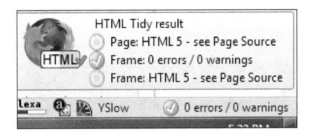

While the following screenshot, shows the result from W3C's online validator for the same `www.packtpub.com` URL:

Errors found while checking this document as HTML5!		
Result:	27 Errors, 2 warning(s)	
Address :	http://www.packtpub.com/	
Encoding :	utf-8	(detect automatically) ▾
Doctype :	HTML5	(detect automatically) ▾
Root Element:	html	
Root Namespace:	http://www.w3.org/1999/xhtml	

The preceding screenshot shows that there are 27 errors and 2 warnings that exist and should be taken care of.

Try W3C's online validator for your own website and try and fix all the errors and warnings shown by this tool.

Reducing DOM elements (Intermediate)

If you are going to have a nicely presented website with a lot of animations, images, and contents, you will surely have thousands of DOM elements to be parsed by web browsers to display the page properly. More the number of DOM elements, more the time it would take to load. So, we need to reduce it to a minimal count through different methods. If your website loads slowly and any event is getting delayed due to JavaScript DOM access, it may happen due to excess number of DOM elements. This can be improved by taking care of and by adjusting HTML tags without hampering the actual content or its functions or display.

How to do it...

Run the following command on Firebug's console under the **Script** tab on whichever website you wish to check the total number of DOM elements:

```
alert(document.getElementsByTagName('*').length);
```

For `Google.com`, it came up to be 325 and for `Aliencoders.com`, it came up to be 2411.

There is scope of eliminating a few unnecessary tags that are not going to participate in the website's content, layout, and functions, such as nested `<div>` and `<span>` tags, which can arrange things properly. This can be done even without making unnecessary nested `div` tags.

If you are using tables or even nested ones, immediately switch to tableless layout with the help of CSS. If any tag is written for comment purposes, we can remove it in our production website.

How it works...

When any web page uses JavaScript or a JavaScript library, such as jQuery, to display the content or to search the content, it would always start the search from the beginning of the DOM elements. More DOM elements would mean you are compromising with the page loading time and patience of the users.

So, when your website's layout is dependent on CSS and JavaScript, which is but obvious in this era, every DOM elements would be matched with CSS to display it in the desired way. So, less DOM elements means spending less time on CSS and JavaScript matching, which will display the page faster to the end users.

 DOM, that is, Document Object Model elements are nothing but HTML tags.

You may try the **YUI** framework (`http://yuilibrary.com/`) for your JavaScript and CSS files provided by Yahoo!.

Setting up CSS sprites (Advanced)

I have already shown how to minimize the file size by combining all images in the *Minimizing HTTP requests (Simple)* recipe. CSS sprites are a kind of advanced version of image maps that uses the CSS technique to handle different images for different purposes from the same big image file. Users usually think that combining all images into one would make the file's size much larger but it is not like that. It will either be the same or smaller than the sum of all individual file sizes.

Getting ready

This tutorial doesn't concentrate on how to make beautiful images and combining all images into one; so, I assume you have the combined image to play with CSS sprites. Almost all major websites (Yahoo!, Google, Amazon, IMBD, and so on) use this technique. If your website deals with a lot of images, you must consider using CSS sprites.

The PageSpeed plugin under Firefox suggests that we combine these images and use CSS sprites, as shown in following screenshot:

> ⚠ ▾ Combine images into CSS sprites
>
> The following images served from aliencoders.com should be combined into as few images as possible using CSS sprites.
>
> - http://www.aliencoders.com/misc/feed.png
> - http://www.aliencoders.com/sites/all/themes/acquia_marina/images/block-gradient.png
> - http://www.aliencoders.com/sites/all/themes/acquia_marina/images/blue-button.png
> - http://www.aliencoders.com/sites/all/themes/acquia_marina/images/content-gradient.png
> - http://www.aliencoders.com/sites/all/themes/acquia_marina/images/green-bullet.png
> - http://www.aliencoders.com/sites/all/themes/acquia_marina/images/rounded-corner-left-right.png
> - http://www.aliencoders.com/sites/all/themes/acquia_marina/images/rounded-corners-search.png
> - http://www.aliencoders.com/sites/all/themes/acquia_marina/images/tab-left.png

How to do it...

1. You should consider wisely which images should be cached and how. You might have various `.png` and `.gif` images; try to combine them all in one. If you have smaller images like icons, try to combine them all into one because it would not just reduce the download size and file size but would reduce the number of HTTP requests.

2. Think about images that are cacheable as discussed under the *Adding an Expires or Cache-Control header (Simple)* recipe. Cacheable images would not have to be downloaded again and again. We can achieve this goal either by doing all the mentioned steps manually by using image-editing tools, such as Adobe Photoshop or logo manager, or we can use online sprite-making tool.

3. If you have made a combined image using Photoshop, before writing CSS code for it, you should find out the height and width of each image using ruler tool in Photoshop, so that you can use its dimension at CSS scripts to make it work properly.

4. You may use **MeasureIt** (https://addons.mozilla.org/en-us/firefox/ addon/measureit/), a Firefox add-on, to find out the exact height and width of the specified chunk of an image, as shown in following screenshot:

5. Let say you have created an image that consists of three small images for each option for three different events in various colors, that is, Home, About, and Contact Us are in the color green at the beginning, but once you hover on any of these three options, say About, it would turn red and when you click on it, it would turn blue. These are not just text but the images which make your website very attractive.

6. Let's assume, you have the following image, which is the combination of two different images and you need to write the CSS sprite code for it, so that it should only show one image at a time. At first, it should show the first button but after clicking on it, it should show the second button. Let's assume the height of each button is 50px and the width of each button is 300px and image name is `sprites.png`, which is at the same place where the CSS script is. This would look like the following screenshot:

Here is the CSS code for it is:

```
ul#button {
    height: 50px;
    list-style: none;
    margin: 0 auto;
    width: 300px;
}

ul#button li#buttonOne a {
    background: url("sprites.png") no-repeat scroll 0 -50px
transparent;
    width: 300px;
}

ul#button li#buttonOne a:active {
    background-position: 0 -50px;
}
```

However, you don't have to go through all such things, such as writing CSS sprites codes, calculating the height and width of each button, and combining all images into one. **SpriteMe** (`http://spriteme.org/`) is an online tool that finds all the images from the web page and combines it into one, re-computes CSS background positions, and generate a CSS sprite for you, which you can use in your web page directly.

Here is the suggested CSS sprite image and suggested CSS code for the `packtpub.com` home page:

7. Click on **make all** to combine all the listed images and then click on **export CSS** to use the modified code. Don't forget to remove the comments and minify before using it on the production site.

There's more...

If you wish to make a combined image sprite using CSS, you should visit the **csssprites** page (`http://csssprites.com/`). If you are going to add or remove a few images time and again, you better have the image in the `.psd` format and play with it. It would save your time; it will be easy to maintain CSS codes for it too. After seeing the CSS code for image sprites, you would clearly notice that, it is best suited for icons or one-time used images on the web page. CSS sprites cannot be used if the image is repeated for more than one time on that web page. Use it wisely and yes, note that the Opera browser has problems with it.

Don't use images that use more than 256 color palettes and avoid `.jpg` images for image sprites. Always prefer `.gif` or `.png` having a transparent background, if possible.

Enabling compression (Simple)

If your website contains numerous JavaScript and CSS files and images, it's better to compress them while sending them over the network. This can be done by enabling gzip, which we will show this recipe.

Getting ready

There are a few things that can't be handled by the website owner or developer, such as the client's Internet speed, ISP, and geographical location, which can affect the speed of any web page. But, programmers can tweak to reduce the file size sent over the network and can reduce the size of the HTTP response that we got under status 200 and 304 in the previous recipe. One simple technique is compressing the file size over the network. That would reduce the time taken to send the HTTP request and get back the HTTP response.

How to do it...

As we cannot control the client's browser whose job is just to send the **Accept-Encoding** attribute to the server with value as `gzip` or `deflate` or `nothing`. So, we have to configure the server so that it will return a zipped/compressed content if the browser is able to handle it, which would ultimately save the bandwidth and the user will feel that site is loading faster.

1. If you are working on IIS, Microsoft's compression link (`http://technet.microsoft.com/en-us/library/cc730629(v=ws.10).aspx`) would help you set the enable compression options through the GUI, step by step.

2. If you are working with the Apache server and have the access to modify the `.htaccess` file, you may try the following lines. Usually, Apache has two compression modes, `mod_deflate` and `mod_gzip`. More details on enabling compression are given in the Apache Online Docs (`http://httpd.apache.org/docs/2.0/mod/mod_deflate.html`).

3. Add these lines to your `.htaccess` file:

```
# compresses text, html, xhtml, rss, javascript, css, xml, json
etc.
AddOutputFilterByType DEFLATE text/plain
AddOutputFilterByType DEFLATE text/html
AddOutputFilterByType DEFLATE text/css
AddOutputFilterByType DEFLATE text/xhtml
AddOutputFilterByType DEFLATE text/xml

# Or compress specific file types:
<files *.html>
SetOutputFilter DEFLATE
</files>

#or use AddOutputFilterByType
AddOutputFilterByType DEFLATE text/html text/plain text/xml
```

4. Apache checks if the browser has sent the **Accept-Encoding** header and according to the request, sends the compressed or uncompressed file back.

    So, first check whether your browser is able to send the **Accept-Encoding** header or not, as shown in the following screenshot:

```
Headers   Response

Response Headers

                        Age  48484
              Cache-Control  public, max-age=691200
           Content-Encoding  gzip
             Content-Length  22368
               Content-Type  text/javascript; charset=UTF-8
                       Date  Thu, 14 Mar 2013 19:39:14 GMT
                    Expires  Fri, 22 Mar 2013 19:39:14 GMT
              Last-Modified  Thu, 14 Mar 2013 03:41:31 GMT
                     Server  sffe
                       Vary  Accept-Encoding
      X-Content-Type-Options  nosniff
            X-XSS-Protection  1; mode=block

Request Headers

                     Accept  text/html,application/xhtml+xml,application/xml;
            Accept-Encoding  gzip, deflate
            Accept-Language  en-us,en;q=0.5
                 Connection  keep-alive
```

5. In case you are not permitted to modify code, you can have the PHP code return the compressed content. Try the following PHP code at the top of your script. Make sure extension is `.php` and not `.html`:

```php
<?php
if (substr_count($_SERVER['HTTP_ACCEPT_ENCODING'], 'gzip')

ob_start("ob_gzhandler");
 else
ob_start();
?>
```

This code checks the **Accept-Encoding** header and returns a zipped version of the file if possible. But try to use Apache to compress the file size at a server level, which would be much faster and efficient.

How it works...

Browsers usually indicate zipping support under the `Accept-Encoding` header as in the HTTP request, **Accept-Encoding**: `gzip, deflate`

After receiving the request, the web server compresses files and notifies the browser by returning the response under the `Content-Encoding` header, that is, **Content-Encoding**: `gzip`.

If you are using Apache 1.3, you should know that it uses the `mod_gzip` (`http://sourceforge.net/projects/mod-gzip/`) module and Apache 2.x uses the `mod_deflate` (`http://httpd.apache.org/docs/2.0/mod/mod_deflate.html`) module for file compression. Compressing images and PDFs don't make any sense as it is already compressed. So, it would be a wastage of server time and memory too.

Optimizing images (Simple)

This recipe will show you how to optimize the website by using optimized images with the help of different techniques and available tools. When you are taking care of every single line of code to make the website consume less bandwidth, load faster without compromising the site's quality, you need to take care of static content as well. Optimizing images is one of them.

How to do it...

1. Avoid the use of images to display text if not necessary. It will consume bandwidth and make your site slower, which your user would not like. For example, no need of images to show FAQ, About Us, and Home links. Simple text with CSS styles would work better.

2. Avoid resizing the image. When you are posting content on the website, which have to show the images, use the original size of that image instead of resizing a bigger image into a smaller one. Your site will load that bigger file size image and slow down your website. So, resize the image into smaller one using photo editor tool like Photoshop.

   Use the `height` and `width` attributes under the `img` tag with the original image's height and width. It will help the browser to load the images in a much faster way:

   ```
   <img width="250" height="250" src="image-path" />
   ```

3. Optimize the image file size by using the correct image format. When you have to use beautiful buttons, tabs, and so on, use CSS codes rather than using various images for this purpose. It will not only slow down your website, but will chock the site bandwidth. As a result the users will not want to wait till all images get loaded and will leave the site even before the main content is shown.

    We need to use the correct image format as per our requirement. If web optimization is the main goal without losing users and quality content, use Photoshop to create high-quality lossless images with smaller size or use any online tool such as **smush.it** (http://smush.it/), which is available as a Firefox extension and even hosted by Yahoo! as a standalone web-based tool.

There's more...

The most common file formats used over the Internet are JPEG, GIF, and PNG.

▸   Use GIF or PNG when you are using smaller images, any animated images, and so on.

▸   As image quality matters apart from website optimization, use JPEG with a lower color palette, that is, around 32 or 64 color palettes.

▸   Try to keep the amount of colors to a minimum and use flat graphics instead of photographs. This way you can create images with palettes of 16 colors, keeping the file size extremely small and fast to download.

Minifying JavaScript and CSS files (Simple)

To load a web page faster, we should minify the scripts used that are responsible for displaying that page and for any event action, that is, minify CSS and JavaScript as much as possible. The process of removing unwanted characters, such as whitespaces, newline, and comment, which don't alter its functionality is termed as **minification**.

Getting ready

Minified code is very efficient and makes the website faster, when deployed over the Internet. Minifying the code is required for JavaScript, CSS, and even HTML.

The compression ratio mostly depends upon the removal of comments, whitespaces, and block delimiters that are used, which may go up to a 60-percent compression ratio in a best scenario.

How to do it...

1. Use external script as much as possible for JavaScript, that is:

   ```
   <script src = "path-to-javascript-files" type = "text/
   javascript"></script>
   ```

   For CSS scripts, use the following code snippet:

   ```
   <link rel="stylesheet" href="path-to-css-file" type="text/css" />
   ```

2. Minify each JavaScript file manually or by using any of the following ways:

   - Using online JavaScript minifier tools such as **JSCompress.com** (http://jscompress.com/), **Packer** (http://dean.edwards.name/packer/).

     In case of CSS scripts, use **csscompressor** (http://www.csscompressor.com/).

   - Using third-party tools such as **yuicompressor** (http://yui.github.com/yuicompressor/) by Yahoo!, Microsoft Ajax Minifier (http://ajaxmin.codeplex.com/) by Microsoft, **jsmin** (http://crockford.com/javascript/jsmin), or **Minify** (http://code.google.com/p/minify/).

     The same works for CSS scripts, with tools used such as **yuicompressor** (http://yui.github.com/yuicompressor/) by Yahoo!, **minify**, and **CSSTidy** (http://csstidy.sourceforge.net/).

3. The last option could be to minify and combine all JavaScript code or CSS script into one file.

When you try to minify CSS it will remove comments, whitespaces, and will merge all duplicate properties. If you use **CSSTidy** to minimize CSS scripts, the following things will be taken care of. For example, consider the following code:

```
a{
   property:x;
   property:y;
}
```

This code becomes a{property:y;}, where all duplicate properties are merged.

Next, consider margin:1px 1px 1px 1px;, which will become margin:1px;.

The rest goes on in the same manner, with margin:0px; becoming margin:0;, a{margin-top:10px; margin-bottom:10px; margin-left:10px; margin-right:10px;} becomes a{margin:10px;}, margin:010.0px; becomes margin:10px;, and so on.

How it works...

We often try to minimize the size of the scripts, which would not only reduce the number of bytes downloaded but would also reduce the number of requests sent to the server, which usually makes it more efficient and loads the page faster.

Let's analyze the web page before minifying any scripts using the browser-plugin **YSlow** (`http://developer.yahoo.com/yslow/`) powered by Yahoo!, which suggests to you the best way to load the web page faster by analyzing all important web optimization factors that we would cover in this book.

I assume that you are using either Firefox or Safari or Opera or Chrome to analyze the web page. On these browsers you will find the YSlow add-on shown at the bottom-right corner with a speedometer icon. Once you click on the icon, you will see something like the following screenshot (I am using Firefox for this purpose):

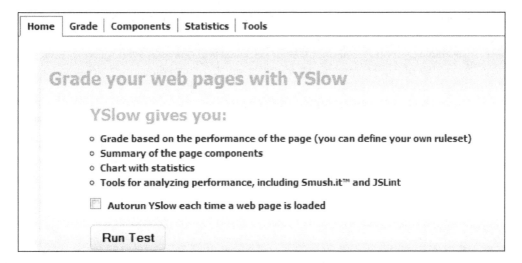

Now, click on **Run Test** to analyze any desired website. I am testing www.aliencoders.com here and the result shows Grade D with all other details, as shown in the following screenshot:

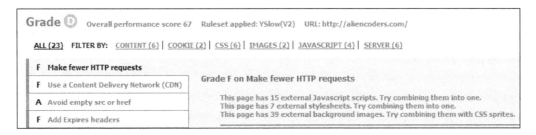

It analyzes the top 23 web optimization techniques and grades them individually. It even suggests solutions to fix such issues.

So, minimize all your JavaScript and CSS files using the previously mentioned steps and combine all JavaScript files into one file and follow the same for all CSS files as well.

The minified jQuery (`http://code.jquery.com/jquery-1.9.1.min.js`) file size is 90.4 KB, while and the simple jQuery (`http://code.jquery.com/jquery-1.9.1.js`) script bears the same content, but with a file size of 271 KB.

There's more...

Minifying scripts has several advantages:

- ▸ Users can quickly download all minified files, which are now smaller in size
- ▸ Bandwidth consumption of the website will be reduced
- ▸ Combining various JavaScript files or CSS files into one single file will also reduce a number of HTTP requests to the server, which in turn will allow more users to access the website faster
- ▸ Comments, whitespaces, block delimiters, and so on are not particularly required for JavaScript or CSS execution, so it will surely enhance execution time by manifolds

Minify will combine multiple CSS or JavaScript files into one CSS or JavaScript file respectively with all other minified concepts being implemented. It even serves them with the `gzip` encoding technique.

The Microsoft Ajax Minifier (`http://ajaxmin.codeplex.com/`) includes the following components:

- ▸ `ajaxmin.exe`: This is a command-line tool for minifying JavaScript files
- ▸ `ajaxmintask.dll`: This is an MSBuild task for minifying JavaScript files in a Visual Studio project
- ▸ `ajaxmin.dll`: This is a component that you can use in your C# or VB.NET applications to minify JavaScript files

You can add the Microsoft Ajax Minifier as a custom MSBuild task to a Visual Studio project, which will allow the user to automatically minify all of the JavaScript files under the mentioned project.

Apart from minimizing JavaScript or CSS, one can even obfuscate the source code but it's a bit complex than minification, and there are more chances that you introduce bugs rather than making an efficient, functional website. So, use the obfuscation technique at your own risk.

Don't confuse the minification technique of the scripts with the more general data compression technique. The minified script can be interpreted and executed immediately without any uncompressing application and interestingly the same interpreter can work with both the original and the minified source, yielding the same result.

Setting up browser caching (Simple)

Web cache is like a middle man between your page and the server from where the page gets fetched. It helps to send static content, for example, CSS, images, and JavaScript directly to the client without sending a request to the server, which ultimately reduces latency and network bandwidth.

Usually caching can be achieved in three ways, caching at browser end, which is called **browser cache** or **private cache**; whereas **proxy cache** also termed as **shared cache** would serve the same cache to as many users as possible to route through them that is, proxy cache. Nowadays **Content Delivery Network (CDN)** is getting popular, which is also used to serve as a cache medium to the users and is also termed as **gateway cache**.

How to do it...

You may increase the cache size and frequency to check the page's freshness, image caching, and so on, by setting the cache option available in all major browsers. I am showing you the same using Mozilla Firefox browser as follows:

1. Open the browser and navigate to **Tools | Options | Advanced**, and then select the **Network** tab to get the following screenshot:

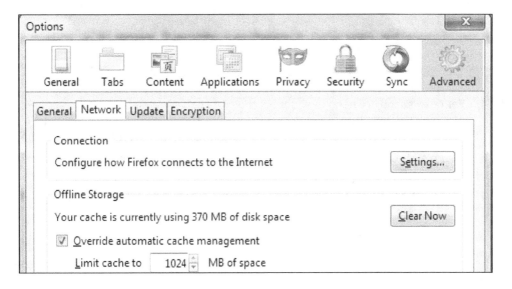

2. If you wish to go ahead and are sure about the config details, check out the `about:config` options for cache. You will see the warning message on doing so, which says, **It might void your warranty!**, just click on the **I'll be careful**, I promise button, and then on the filter box type cache. Now, you may change the browser cache disk space size, the **check_doc_frequency** setting, and so on.

> For **browser.cache.check_doc_frequency**, the default value is **3**. You can use 0 to 3 where:
>
> 0 means to check for a new version of a page once per session
>
> 1 means to check for a new version every time a page is loaded
>
> 2 mean never check for a new version, always load the page from cache
>
> 3 means to check for a new version when the page is out-of-date, which by default exists

3. Change the config settings at your own risk as shown in the following screenshot:

Preference Name	Status	Type	Value
browser.cache.check_doc_frequency	default	integer	3
browser.cache.disk.capacity	user set	integer	1048576
browser.cache.disk.enable	default	boolean	true
browser.cache.disk.max_entry_size	default	integer	51200
browser.cache.disk.smart_size.enabled	default	boolean	true
browser.cache.disk.smart_size.first_run	user set	boolean	false
browser.cache.disk.smart_size_cached_value	user set	integer	1048576
browser.cache.disk_cache_ssl	default	boolean	true
browser.cache.memory.enable	default	boolean	true
browser.cache.memory.max_entry_size	default	integer	5120
browser.cache.offline.capacity	default	integer	512000
browser.cache.offline.enable	default	boolean	true
browser.taskbar.previews.cachetime	default	integer	5

(about:config — Filter: cache)

4. For proxy cache, we need to either set the proxy server details to our browser ISPs, already save them through routers and firewalls that we can directly use, or just use interception proxy to figure out automatically, which proxy server to use for caching.

5. For gateway cache, webmasters are responsible to set up the correct cache settings to use the CDN's properties efficiently. Everything is customized and user friendly, one just needs to use their services. Famous gateway cache servers are Akamai and AWS.

6. We can set a cache-control header and expires to make them working as we discussed it in the *Adding an Expires or Cache-Control header (Simple)* recipe. If you are using the Apache server, use mod_expires and mod_headers for this purpose as follows:

```
### activate mod_expires
ExpiresActive On
ExpiresByType image/gif seconds
```

7. In CGI-Perl, you may write cache-control as follows:

```
print "Cache-Control: max-age = 3600\n";
```

How it works...

As we have manually set so many rules of web cache and few are already implemented under HTTP 1.0 and HTTP 1.1, whenever a page is requested, it would check the following things to decide to cache it or not:

▶ If the header response sends any cache-control parameters to have cache, it will serve from the cache and save the cache for future use.

▶ If the request is authenticated or secure like HTTPS, make sure it isn't cached.

▶ A cached material will be server, if the cache checker or content-header for expires max-age is way ahead.

▶ You might have observed that sometimes there is no Internet connection, but still you are able to browse pages hence and forth. This is what the magic of cached stuff.

▶ If no cache-control or expires or ETags headers is present, it is not meant to be cached indirectly.

Browser cache helps you by not sending the request to the server again when you click on the **Back** button. But if it's a login page or any transaction secured page, it must revalidate. So, use the cache settings carefully according to the page requirements.

Using Apache mod_pagespeed – installing and configuring (Advanced)

Do you want to make your website much faster by making minimum changes to the code? If yes, use Apache's mod_pagespeed module, which will take care of web optimization best practices automatically after properly setting up and configuring.

Getting ready

Before diving deep into this module, let's analyze your website score using Google's page analysis online tool, which will not only check all the best practices to make your website faster, but will provide you detailed information about what changes are needed to make it more responsive and fast. Check the following URL: `https://developers.google.com/speed/pagespeed/insights`.

The preceding URL will show you a textbox where you need to enter your website name and click on **ANALYZE**, as shown in the following screenshot:

After a few seconds, it will give you a score on a scale of 100 and on the left you can find the suggestion list categorized by the priority level.

For Alien Coders, it is 90 out of 100, with some suggestions for best practices, as shown in the following screenshot:

How to do it...

There are a lot of things to do with this module, which we can't just explain as it requires another book to explain it fully with real-life examples. We will try to cover the basic things to get started with. So, `mod_pagespeed` is an Apache 2.x module, which is added into an existing Apache server with the help of the `pagespeed.cong` configure file. Here, we will deal only with the basics of installing and configuring the `mod_pagespeed` module. You may explore the rest of the work easily after that as follows:

1. Install `mod_pagespeed`. Currently it supports only:

    ❑   CentOS/Fedora (32 bit and 64 bit)

    ❑   Debian/Ubuntu (32 bit and 64 bit)

2. So, to install it on Debian or Ubuntu, please run the following command, make sure you are as root:

    ```
    pkg -i mod-pagespeed-*.deb apt-get -f install
    ```

3. To install it on CentOS or Fedora, please execute the following commands as a root:

    ```
    yum install at # In case you don't have "at" installed which
       is required to download rpm package
    rpm -U mod-pagespeed-*.rpm
    ```

 As it is from the Google code repository and they maintain it, so it's a good idea to let it update automatically if any updates are available there. So by default, the Google repository will be added to your system.

4. So it installs `mod_pagespeed.so` for Apache 2.2 and `mod_pagespeed_ap24.so` for Apache 2.4, upgradable configuration files `pagespeed.conf, pagespeed_libraries.conf` in Fedora, and `pagespeed.load` on Debian provided you don't change these files ever and JavaScript minifier `pagespeed_js_minify`

    ```
    mod_pagespeed Configuration
    ```

5. The `mod_pagespeed` configuration directives should be wrapped inside an `IfModule` module as follows:

    ```
    <IfModule pagespeed_module>#config lines here</IfModule>
    ```

6. An example of the `mod_pagespeed` configuration that can be used as a guideline is as follows:

```
# This page shows statistics about the mod_pagespeed
# module.
<Location /mod_pagespeed_statistics>
Order allow, deny
# One may insert other "Allow from" lines to add hosts that
# are allowed to look at generated statistics. Another
# possibility is to comment out the "Order" and "Allow"
# options from the config file, to allow any client that
# can reach the server to examine statistics. This might be
# appropriate in an experimental setup or if the Apache
# server is protected by a reverse proxy that will filter
# URLs to avoid exposing these statistics, which may reveal
# site metrics that not be shared otherwise.
Allow from localhost
Allow from 127.0.0.
SetHandler mod_pagespeed_statistics
</Location>
```

7. The output filter is used to parse, optimize, and re-serialize HTML content that is generated elsewhere in the Apache server as follows:

```
# Direct Apache to send all HTML output to the
# mod_pagespeed output handler.
AddOutputFilterByType MOD_PAGESPEED_OUTPUT_FILTER text/html
```

8. It is noteworthy to mention that `mod_pagespeed` automatically enables `mod_deflate` for compression.

   - ❑ To turn `mod_pagespeed` on, insert at the top line of `pagespeed.conf`: `ModPagespeed on`
   - ❑ To turn it off, just write `ModPagespeed off`
   - ❑ To disable it permanently, write `ModPagespeed unplugged`

How it works...

You just need to install `mod_pagespeed` properly for the first time and need to remember how to disable or enable it. That's it. The rest of the configuration settings that set filters are already set at the best for your website by Google developers. If you wish to explore more and want to make settings, configurations, and filters according to your requirements, you must go through the PageSpeed documentation provided by Google.

Once Apache gets started and you start to visit any website, send the PageSpeed statistics to the `stats` folder. By default, it will set the localhost to **127.0.0.1**, but you can allow more sites as per your needs.

There's more...

If you host a website and have no control over `mod_pagespeed`, try the browser's plugin from `https://developers.google.com/speed/pagespeed/`,and perform the following steps:

1. Check **Download link** at the right-bottom corner for Firefox and Chrome.

2. Once you download the plugin and restart your browser, open any website to analyze the speed. Then press _F12_ to turn on the plugin, select the **PageSpeed** tab, and click on **Run Analyze**.

3. Once that is done, you will be able to see something like the following screenshot, which will explain all the errors, warnings, and remedies for the given site:

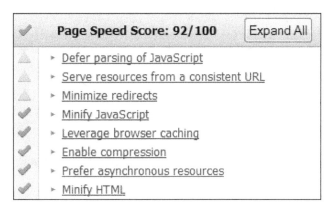

4. Click on the text **Expand All**, as shown in the preceding screenshot to see all the suggestions listed by Google to make the website much more faster and efficient.

Making favicon.ico small and cacheable (Simple)

An icon that you see over the top of the browser at the left corner is called **favicon**, that is, favorite icon.

If you carefully observe the root directory of your website, you will find that `favicon.ico` is residing there by default. If it's not there, it would always throw an error to the server that `favicon.ico` was not found with the HTTP status code 404, which we don't want to happen. So, either handle such status code or better have one small favicon in your root directory. We need it anyhow because modern browsers always look for it.

How to do it...

1. Your hosting service provider would provide one by default, else you can create your own by using any icon generator tool or the freely available online icon generator (`http://tools.dynamicdrive.com/favicon/`).

2. When you open the preceding link, you will see the following screenshot:

3. Click on **Browse...** as shown in the preceding screenshot to create an icon. You can click on those **Optional** checkboxes, else it will be 16 x 16 pixels by default.

4. Then click on **Create Icon**. You will see the **Download Favicon** button, as shown in the following screenshot:

5. Click on the **Download Favicon** button to download the `favicon.ico` file, as shown in the following screenshot:

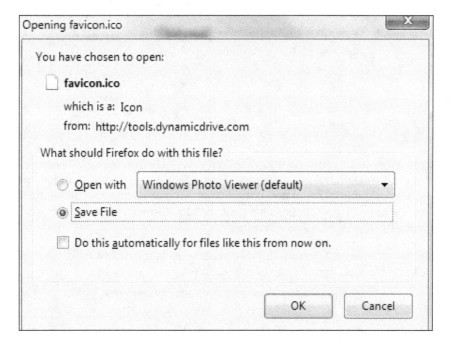

6. Now, click on **OK** to save it; upload the file on the website under the `root` directory, and you are done.

 Make sure it is of 16 x 16 or 32 x 32 or 48 x 48 or 64 x 64 pixels and very small in size, say less than 1 KB. Most of the websites use 16 x 16 pixels to display favicon, so better use the same for your website too.

How it works...

Whenever you hit the page, it sends requests to the server, and all the files get downloaded either from the server or cache depending upon the expires header. By default, favicon will always get downloaded whenever you are making a request to the server, so as to avoid any delay and its interference with downloading other files from the server.

Try to have the favicon in the root directory with a size less than 1 KB and try to have it in the `.ico` format, and set the expires header to a future date. If you are going to change the extension of your favicon, be sure to use the `<link>` tag in HTML. For example:

```
<link rel = "shortcut icon" href = "/images/favicon.gif"
  type = "image/x-icon" />
```

This following screenshot shows the grade of the favicon image in a website using the YSlow plugin in Firefox:

> **Grade A on Make favicon small and cacheable**
>
> Favicon is more than 2000 bytes

There's more...

YSlow suggests that one should manually create a cacheable favicon, so let's always do it. Almost every modern browser (tested on Firefox 9, IE9, and Opera10) requests a `favicon.ico` by default, unless and until you are not mentioning your own customized shortcut icon via the `<link>` tag. So, it's a good idea to always have the favicon.ico file in your root directory, to avoid a **File not found** error.

- You can create your own customized favicon using the online tool from `http://tools.dynamicdrive.com/favicon/`.

- If you use Photoshop heavily for image manipulation, you may use a Photoshop plugin (`http://download.cnet.com/Icon-Plugin-for-PhotoShop/3000-2195_4-10587858.html`) for an icon image creation that is available for free.

- There are two famous paid tools available over the Internet, which does the icon creation job in a more professional and easier way:

    - The first one is Axialis IconWorkshop (`http://download.cnet.com/Axialis-IconWorkshop/3000-2195_4-10124592.html?tag=contentBody;`)

    - The other one is Icon Packager (`http://download.cnet.com/IconPackager/3000-2195_4-10031210.html`)

Avoiding redirects and Not Found errors – 301 and 404 codes (Advanced)

You might have observed that you opened one URL, but were being redirected to another URL. Like when you try to open `http://www.google.com/docs`, you would be redirected to `https://drive.google.com/#my-drive`.

Sometimes it is necessary to do so due to various possible reasons as follows:

- To show temporarily moved article with a hint that it has been moved temporarily
- To show the content even if the URL is permanently moved through aliased URL
- To display easily remembered URL
- To add a trailing slash to make the website working fine if not configured properly on server side
- To transfer URL from HTTP to HTTPS or vice versa according to the client's requirement
- To display the domain name based on geolocation like typing `google.com` would redirect you to `google.co.in` if you are in India

Whichever the case may be, if you don't have any choice, go for the redirect option, else try to minimize it in your website.

If you have changed the content's URL recently using different rewrite engine rules or by any other way, try to fix the broken link, which will be a waste of time and we could lose users as well.

How to do it...

There are various ways to minimize or avoid redirects. Let's see how to avoid redirects as follows:

1. If you know the exact URL for any content, type that even though it is a bit lengthy. Trust me, it would save your time, and the response would be much faster because latency period while redirecting the URL is not present there. The worst thing about redirecting a URL is that unless and until it is being redirected properly it will not render anything, not even a single line of that page.

2. Sometimes a wrongly typed URL also redirects you to the correctly indented page like `http://www.facebook.net` would lead you to `https://www.facebook.com/`, so better type the correct URL, if possible.

3. Try to type the forward slash (/) at the end of URL to render the default page properly like `http://www.aliencoders.com/` to open the default page that is, `http://www.aliencoders.com/index.html`, which would otherwise give an error if it's not properly handled by the server. You may rewrite the rule to avoid redirect in such a case, so that the server automatically corrects the URL and serves the right resource for you.

4. Many websites use redirect to log the user's information for web analytics; if it is necessary or required, use some other method, such as sending a request through JavaScript, which should be negligible and the user would not notice the latency. For example:

```
img.src = "http://www.example.com/logs/small.gif?page = " +
    encodeURI(thisPage) + "&ref = " + encodeURI(referPage);
```

5. Now to avoid showing bad requests or repair broken links, it is quite obvious that URLs should be mentioned from time to time or article's reference would not work, because of a broken link, which may happen due to removal of such content or moving of such content somewhere else. We should check broken links and fix them, if we find any, from time to time. **Top 'page not found' errors** at www.aliencoders.com with the count is shown in the following screenshot:

Top 'page not found' errors	
Count ▼	Message
472	forum/index.php
425	comment/reply/forum
329	reply/forum
329	comment/reply/857
256	
199	comment/reply/blog
191	reply/blog

How it works...

When you pass any previously mentioned URLs for redirection, then it is either already mentioned at the server sided with the help of rewrite engine rule or it uses the `http-equiv="refresh"` mechanism at the client side. As I always insist, try to avoid redirects; but if it is worthy to use redirects, use the server-side techniques to use redirects.

When you open any webpage, which is moved permanently or not available over the Internet, you would get either **404 (Not Found) error** or **410 (Gone) error** as the server response. If you are not looking over these two issues seriously, you are surely playing with the user's emotions for which you have to pay by losing them permanently.

There's more...

Wherever possible, you should update the links to resources that have moved, or delete those links if the resources have been removed. Avoid using HTTP redirects to send users to the requested resources, or to serve a substitute suggestion page. As previously described, redirects also slow down your site, and are better to avoid as much as possible. Use Google Analytics or any such famous analytics to track down all these errors to avoid it as much as possible.

Using the Flush method (Intermediate)

Why to wait for the response from the server, if we can render the frontend script in between. Here, the Flush method comes into picture.

Getting ready

Did you ever observe that some websites take a fraction of seconds to start displaying the content, whereas few websites, such as Google or Facebook start displaying the content like a flash?

This happens when a dynamic page is waiting for the server's response to display the HTML page. During that time browsers remain idle, which you can observe easily. We can use the flush method to download all CSS, JavaScript, and other content mentioned in the header and the browser can start displaying the partial content of the body part at the same time, so the user will feel that the site is a bit faster. This trick is beneficial for those websites where lots of backend requests are sent or frontend is having less content to display.

How to do it...

A good place to consider flushing is right after the head, because the HTML for the head is usually easier to produce and it allows you to include any CSS and JavaScript files for the browser to start fetching in parallel, while the backend is still processing. For example:

```
PHP: <?php flush(); ?>
```

It is not much effective though, but considering this fact one should consider flushing the buffer after the `</head>` tag, for example:

```
</head>
<?php flush(); //flushed to display content from body part ?>
<body>
```

How it works...

Although there are lots of conditions to load a web page faster. It depends upon the server's response of how fast it can send you the HTML output and how fast it can send you all the files mentioned under the <head> tag. So, flushing the buffer before the <body> tag is a good idea to make the process faster at the server end, which makes the whole process faster and productive.

Flushing in PHP usually may happen in the following circumstances:

- If the PHP interpreter found the end of the page
- If the buffer exceeds the number of bytes specified under the PHP configuration setting
- If the PHP's flush-related functions are called, such as flush() and ob_flush()

 Programming languages, such as PHP, Perl, Python, ASP, and Ruby, contain a flush function.

In any programming language, the concept of flushing the buffer is the same and that is writing the contents of reserved areas of memory to the hard disk. This way you will achieve faster response without breaking anything.

Configuring ETags (Advanced)

Entity tags (**ETags**) is the way to determine that the contents available in the browser's cache is the same or different from the origin server.

ETags treats the CSS, JavaScript, and image files as entities, and provides a mechanism to validate the specific version of a component/entity that is returned from the server side under the response header as ETag: "some-value". Notice that it is stringified before sending the value to the client. Now, the server specifies the component's ETag using the ETag response header that changes it or has the same string value as of the previous one.

Now, if the browser has to check and validate the entity, it uses the If-None-Match request header to pass the ETag back to the server and in return the server responds with either 200 or 304 status code. If it returns **304 HTTP Code**, the content has not been modified and saved some KBs to get downloaded.

How to do it...

1. If it's the static content, it is easy to calculate the ETag by returning the recent modified date, so that if you update it and being requested by the browser; it would send **HTTP code 200** and will send the updated one.

2. But, if it's a dynamic file whose content changes frequently depending upon the argument and dynamic values, just sending the recent modified date would not be enough to calculate the ETag value. You may use PHP to generate ETag or any dynamic language would do that depending upon your requirement. Apache server automatically configures the ETag values.

3. If all the files are going to be served from the same server, ETAG is important, else it should be disabled in case of CDN.

4. Once can Set/Enable ETags using Apache's config file that is, `httpd.conf` or `apache2.conf` (depends upon which Apache version you are using) and add the following line at the end of the file:

   `FileETag INode MTime Size`

   Here, `INode`, `MTimes`, and `Size` mean:

   ▶ `INode`: This shows the file's i-node number in the calculation
   ▶ `MTime`: This shows the date and time the file was last modified on
   ▶ `Size`: This shows the number of bytes of the file

5. If you are using a cluster of servers, better disable it by adding the following lines in `httpd.conf` or `apache2.conf` at the end of this file:

   `FileETag None`
   `Header unset ETag`

6. In case, it is misconfigured either by mistake of a programmer or web master, it would not show the `If-None-Match` tag under the request header. YSlow under Firefox shows that there are three files present in the site, which have misconfigured ETags.

> **Grade D on Configure entity tags (ETags)**
>
> There are 3 components with misconfigured ETags
>
> • http://s7.addthis.com/js/250/addthis_widget.js#async=1
> • https://api.iflychat.com/asset/poweroff.png
> • http://www.squid-cache.org/Artwork/SN.png

How it works...

The process of requesting, configuring, and matching ETags can be explained with the step-by-step browser-server communication as follows:

1. The user requests a web page, say abc.com, through the browser.

2. The browser sends a request to the server to check and verify the freshness of the content.

3. The server sends the output of a page of abc.com with the value of ETags as strings for the present page.

4. The client gets the content and displays it after caching it with the ETags value for that page with the status code 200, if it's fresh content, as shown in the following screenshot:

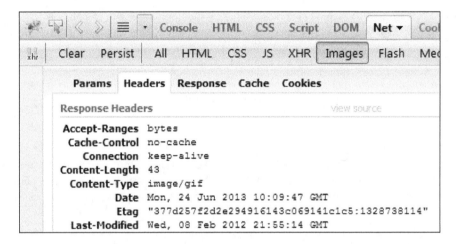

5. The client once again sends a request to the origin server by passing the previously sent ETags value through the If-None-Match tag.

6. The server tests and verifies that the content has not been modified since the last time it was requested and sends a response as 304 status code with a 0 KB file size, as it is already in cache, as shown in the following screenshot:

There's more...

The concept of ETags may not work in the CDN services as it will get the ETag version from one server and the next time it would request to compare it with the others. There is little relief for you if you are using Apache, which is a major role player in the server domain, or IIS then by default, both embed data to the ETag header, which will reduce the chance of a failure on testing and verifying ETags even when coming from different servers.

Making AJAX cacheable (Intermediate)

To improve performance, it's important to optimize these AJAX responses. The most important way to improve the performance of AJAX is to make the responses cacheable. Usually we use AJAX to send data asynchronously to the server and display the result that we get from the server without making the users wait (or less time to wait in practical) for data. We can make it faster if we know that the user is going to ask for the same thing again, then we can make AJAX cacheable. It is almost same as HTTP caching that we have seen in the *Setting up browser caching (Simple)* recipe.

How to do it...

We can make AJAX cacheable by adding the Expires header to the file, which would be called by AJAX as mentioned in the *Adding an Expires or Cache-Control header (Simple)* recipe. We can optimize the AJAX response even by minifying the script, which uses the AJAX calls as discussed in the *Minifying JavaScript and CSS files (Simple)* recipe, and even compress those files that is, GZIP or deflate, as shown in the *Enabling compression (Simple)* recipe.

1. When you set the ETag value and set Apache to avoid redirects, it also applies on all such scripts and AJAX calls, which are going to use those web pages, so it is optimized anyways by following those methods. The following response headers are used to make your AJAX cacheable:

   - **Expires**: This header should be set to an appropriate time in the future depending on how often the content changes. The **Expires** header allows the browser to re-use the cached content for a period of time and avoid any unnecessary round-trips to the server.

   - **Last-Modified**: By using the **Last-Modified** value, the browser can use to check its locally cached content used in the GET method. The server would respond with a 304 status code if the data has not changed.

   - **Cache-Control**: One should set the **Cache-Control** value to `Public`, to store and share the content with other users. It also enables the caching of HTTPS requests in the Firefox browser.

2. If the AJAX response data is user specific, it should not have **Cache-Control** as `Public`. This should be done carefully.

3. You can add these three entities to any files, which are going to be requested under the GET method using Apache settings or using any one of your favorite web programming languages, such as Perl, Python, or PHP. It is being discussed in detail in the *Setting up browser caching (Simple)* recipe.

4. Once the AJAX request is called, you will see `x-requested-with:` `XMLHttpRequest` under the headers sent section and you will also see the three entities mentioned previously under the headers received, as shown in the following screenshot:

Cache-Control	`max-age=31536000, private`
Connection	`keep-alive`
Content-Length	`17258`
Content-Type	`application/x-javascript`
Date	`Tue, 25 Jun 2013 09:32:49 GMT`
Etag	`"436a-4a29909907240"`
Expires	`Wed, 25 Jun 2014 09:32:49 GMT`
Last-Modified	`Fri, 06 May 2011 10:34:41 GMT`

5. AJAX caching would not work if you use the POST method in your AJAX requests, because POST requests are never cached. But, you should always use the POST method if your AJAX request has side effects, for example, moving money between bank accounts.

How it works...

One of the classic examples of AJAX is the autocompletion feature, which you might have experienced while filling any AJAX-enabled online form or might have tried to type e-mail in compose mail and it would display all the user names that match your keystrokes.

Let's take an example of Yahoo! Mail. A user opens the web mail and tries to search for a contact from the address book. Now the browser would look if the address book has been modified since the user's last visit or not; if it has been modified, the browser requests for a new address book before searching for it, else returns the same address book without even requesting the Yahoo! Mail server.

How does it happen? It's simple, browsers need to send the previously accessed address book's timestamp; if this matches, it means the address book has not been modified since that time, so no need to send a request to the server.

There's more...

One more thing worth mentioning in this section is trying to send the GET method instead of POST when sending the AJAX request, which would send the header and the content data together. Be sure to use lesser size; IE doesn't support more than 2 KB of request. If you have to send more than 2 KB data, which is hardly going to happen unless and until you are trying to do some unethical work, use the POST method.

Rules for using the CSS, JavaScript, and image files (Simple)

There are many other ways to enhance web response, which can't fit any of those listed recipes appropriately, so we will discuss such possibilities in this recipe.

How to do it...

We may accomplish it by performing the following steps:

1. **Using external files for stylesheets and JavaScript**: This not only saves bandwidth and loads faster, but helps in caching those files too, which would be impossible if we made it inline.

2. **Using correct order of stylesheets, scripts, and inline JavaScript code**: This will save a lot of download time and make web response even faster.

3. **Don't scale images in HTML**: Scaling images into smaller ones never helps you to reduce the download size or reduce the file size, then why to use bigger images and then use scaling.

4. **Removing Duplicate scripts**: Using the same script time and again is not just a waste of time, but it makes the site heavier by adding unnecessary bits and if that contains a lot of scripts, you can imagine the frustration of the end user.

5. **Avoid CSS @import**: `@import` in CSS is used to import the mentioned CSS files, which adds the extra bit of seconds in loading the page.

6. **Avoiding empty image SRC**: Sending requests to the server for anything unworthy is just the wastage of bandwidth, time, and space of the web page, which may not be welcomed by users.

How it works...

For using externals files for stylesheets and JavaScript, refer to the following points:

▶ If you want to make your web page load faster, from now onwards consider using all the CSS and JavaScript files externally. When you use everything inline, then every time a page gets refreshed, it loads every bit of code from scratch. But using external files give you the opportunity to make it cached, so that on page load it would be served from the cache at the minimal latency and thus reduce the file size and also consume less bandwidth.

▶ It is very useful for the site that uses uniform pattern for every web page. For example, consider any popular **Content Management System** (**CMS**), for example, Drupal, WordPress, Joomla!, and so on. They have uniform CSS and JavaScript patterns and use it for almost every web page, which makes it faster by using this technique and caching these external files and scripts.

For using correct order of styles and scripts, refer to the following points:

▶ It is the web developers' responsibility to include both the CSS and JavaScript files in the correct order to make the website faster. If any JavaScript is mentioned before the CSS files or the Meta tag, it will block other files to download simultaneously, which will slow down the website.

▶ Let's assume a website sends a lot of requests to the server and can download four files simultaneously; in this case, you should use the order wisely to use the simultaneous download properties, which are being chocked by the JavaScript files if encountered in between. The following code shows how the Meta tag, the CSS files, and JavaScript have been wrongly written, which could be modified to make the website response faster:

```
<link rel = "EditURI" type = "application/rsd+xml" title =
  "RSD" href = "http://www.aliencoders.com/blogapi/rsd"/>
<meta property = "fb:app_id" content = "180767955291621"/>
<script type = 'text/javascript' src =
  '//s7.addthis.com/js/250/addthis_widget.js#async =
    1'></script>
<link rel = "alternate" type = "application/rss+xml" title
  = "Alien Coders  RSS" href =
    "http://www.aliencoders.com/rss.xml"/>
<link rel = "shortcut icon" href =
  "/sites/default/files/acquia_marina_favicon.gif" type =
    "image/x-icon"/>
<meta name = "keywords" content =
  "aliencoders, technical website, site for students,
    site for professionals"/>
<link rel = "canonical" href =
  "http://www.aliencoders.com/"/>
<meta property = "og:url" content =
  "http://www.aliencoders.com/"/>
<meta name = "revisit-after" content = "1 day"/>
```

- It is designed usually so that each host can have six parallel connections to download the mentioned files. Let's say there are four CSS files and two JavaScript files and each file takes 20 milliseconds to get downloaded properly. If JavaScript is mentioned above the CSS files, it would take 20 milliseconds to download the first JavaScript file, then the second JavaScript would take 20 milliseconds, and only then will it start downloading the rest of the four CSS files simultaneously in another 20 milliseconds, which sum up to 60 milliseconds to download all the files.

- But, if we reorder the code in such a way that all the CSS files would lay above the JavaScript files, and if you follow the rule of HTML standards mentioned in the *Following HTML standards (Simple)* recipe, the modified code would look like this:

```
<meta name = "keywords" content = "aliencoders, technical
  website, site for students, site for professionals"/>
<meta property = "og:url"
  content = "http://www.aliencoders.com/"/>
<meta name = "revisit-after" content = "1 day"/>
<link rel = "shortcut icon" href = "marina_favicon.gif"
  type = "image/x-icon"/>
<link rel = "alternate" type = "application/rss+xml"
  title = "Alien Coders RSS"
    href = "http://www.aliencoders.com/rss.xml"/>
<link rel = "canonical"
  href = "http://www.aliencoders.com/" />
<link type = "text/css" rel = "stylesheet" media = "all"
  href = "css-file.css"/>
<script type = 'text/javascript'
  src = 'javascript-file.js'></script>
```

- And now assume those four CSS files are at the top and then those two JavaScript files are mentioned, it would download the four CSS files and one JavaScript file simultaneously in 20 milliseconds (as it can't start another JavaScript in parallel because while downloading JavaScript, it doesn't allow any more parallel download) and then the last JavaScript file will get downloaded in 20 milliseconds, which means you saved 20 milliseconds just by reordering the files and scripts properly. If you have any inline JavaScript, put it at the end to evaluate, if possible.

The following section helps you with removing duplicate scripts:

- Sometimes it happens that by mistake or by erroneous code implementation few scripts or CSS files would be loaded more than once due to bad coding, which would do nothing other than causing harm to your sites by not only making the users irate, but by slowing it down tremendously. In any case, you need to avoid it, either by manually inspecting the working code or using any programming language to check for the existence of scripts. If it's there, it does nothing else but load that script.

```
if(exists "$file"){//do nothing and move forward}
else {load_script($file)}
```

To avoid using CSS `@import`, the following points can be considered:

▸ `@import` is a property in CSS to include other related CSS files that just imports those included CSS files, which are doing no good but adding extra bits of seconds in getting to that web page.

▸ The simple thing is, instead of parallel download from one host is getting violated here when `@import` is being called, which just says pause to other downloads until it gets downloaded first, which you don't want for sure and it surely is going to add extra round-trip times to that web page. For example, if `male.css` contains the following content: `@import url("female.css")`, the browser would first download and fully parse the male CSS file before downloading the female CSS file.

▸ I would suggest you to use the `<link>` tag and forget about anything like the `@import` annotation properties in CSS unless and until you have to attend an interview as a CSS expert. It will allow parallel download to the `female.css` file too, which would reduce round-trip time and the page would get loaded faster. For example:

```
<link rel = "stylesheet" href = "first.css">
<link rel = "stylesheet" href = "second.css">
```

To avoid empty image SRC, the following points may help:

▸ Do you want to corrupt the user's data, which you track or maintain at your server log? Do you want to increase the page loading time unnecessarily? If the answer to both is yes, God bless you; otherwise stop using empty SRC either in the HTML or CSS or JavaScript codes.

▸ Never write the code as follows:

```
<img src = ""> or background-image: url("");
or var img = new Image();
img.src = "";
```

▸ It will send an extra request to either the same directory where the page is or requests for the same page again and again when encountered with an empty image SRC in IE, Chrome, and Safari. Firefox and Opera have fixed this issue though, but never ever use an empty image SRC in your life.

▸ For more details on it, check RFC 3986 (`http://www.ietf.org/rfc/rfc3986.txt`); especially sections 5.2 and 5.4.

About Packt Publishing

Packt, pronounced 'packed', published its first book "*Mastering phpMyAdmin for Effective MySQL Management*" in April 2004 and subsequently continued to specialize in publishing highly focused books on specific technologies and solutions.

Our books and publications share the experiences of your fellow IT professionals in adapting and customizing today's systems, applications, and frameworks. Our solution based books give you the knowledge and power to customize the software and technologies you're using to get the job done. Packt books are more specific and less general than the IT books you have seen in the past. Our unique business model allows us to bring you more focused information, giving you more of what you need to know, and less of what you don't.

Packt is a modern, yet unique publishing company, which focuses on producing quality, cutting-edge books for communities of developers, administrators, and newbies alike. For more information, please visit our website: www.packtpub.com.

Writing for Packt

We welcome all inquiries from people who are interested in authoring. Book proposals should be sent to author@packtpub.com. If your book idea is still at an early stage and you would like to discuss it first before writing a formal book proposal, contact us; one of our commissioning editors will get in touch with you.

We're not just looking for published authors; if you have strong technical skills but no writing experience, our experienced editors can help you develop a writing career, or simply get some additional reward for your expertise.

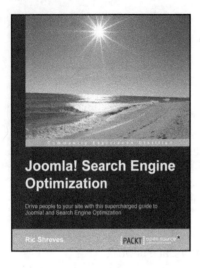

Joomla! Search Engine Optimization

ISBN: 978-1-84951-876-5   Paperback: 116 pages

Drive people to your site with this supercharged guide to Joomla! and Search Optimization

1. Learn how to create a search engine-optimized Joomla! website.

2. Packed full of tips to help you develop an appropriate SEO strategy.

3. Discover the right configurations and extensions for SEO purposes.

Drupal Search Engine Optimization

ISBN: 978-1-84951-878-9   Paperback: 116 pages

Drive people to your site with this supercharged guide to Drupal SEO

1. Learn how to create a search engine-optimized Drupal website.

2. Packed full of tips to help you develop an appropriate SEO strategy.

3. Discover the right configurations and extensions for SEO purposes.

Please check **www.PacktPub.com** for information on our titles

PUBLISHING

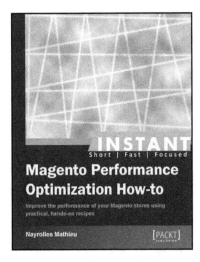

Instant Magento Performance Optimization How-to

ISBN: 978-1-78216-542-2   Paperback: 56 pages

Improve the performance of your Magento stores using practical, hands-on recipes

1. Learn something new in an Instant! A short, fast, focused guide delivering immediate results.

2. Tune your Magento installation for optimal performance.

3. Identify misconfigurations that can cause slow down.

4. Prepare your installation for clustering.

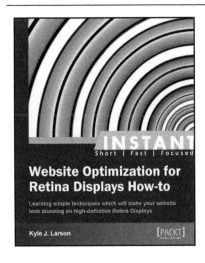

Instant Website Optimization for Retina Displays How-to

ISBN: 978-1-84969-512-1   Paperback: 56 pages

Learning simple techniques which will make your website look stunning on high-defination Retina Displays

1. Learn something new in an Instant! A short, fast, focused guide delivering immediate results.

2. Create high-resolution graphics for websites.

3. Learn to create scalable graphics using CSS, SVG, and Canvas.

Please check **www.PacktPub.com** for information on our titles

www.ingramcontent.com/pod-product-compliance
Lightning Source LLC
LaVergne TN
LVHW080105070326

832902LV00014B/2427